A CLEAN WATER POND; A LONG, SAFE LIFE

By Adriana Diaz-Donoso

Illustrated by Jovan Carl Segura

Library For All Ltd.

LIBRARY FOR ALL

DIGITAL EDUCATION · FOR THE WORLD

Library For All is an Australian not for profit organisation with a mission to make knowledge accessible to all via an innovative digital library solution. Visit us at libraryforall.org

A Clean Water Pond; A Long, Safe Life

This edition published 2022

Published by Library For All Ltd
Email: info@libraryforall.org
URL: libraryforall.org

Library For All gratefully acknowledges the contributions of all who made previous editions of this book possible.

Original illustrations by Jovan Carl Segura

A Clean Water Pond; A Long, Safe Life
Diaz-Donoso, Adriana
ISBN: 978-1-922827-44-9
SKU02661

A CLEAN WATER POND;
A LONG, SAFE LIFE

Uncle José went to visit Ali's new house. He was very happy when he saw the nice pond the family had close to their house.

"It is very nice to swim in the pond," Ali said. "My friends and I like to play there, too."

"Good!" Uncle José said. But then he looked at Ali with a very serious face and added, "I hope you know how to keep the pond clean. Do you know how to do that?"

Ali was very confused and asked, "Uncle José, aren't all ponds clean and safe?"

Uncle José replied, "No! There are many ponds that are contaminated, and if you swim there you can get very sick."

"Contaminated?" Ali asked.
"Yes," Uncle Jose continued.
"Ponds, rivers and streams
are contaminated when
people urinate in their
waters, and if you swim
in those waters you can
get very, very sick."

"Oh, I understand now, Uncle José. We keep the pond clean if we urinate in latrines and very far from the pond," said Ali. "Yes, you are very smart, Ali. I am so proud of you," said Uncle José.

"I will tell my friends what you just said, Uncle José, because I want the pond to be clean and safe. Then we can continue swimming and having fun there. Thanks for your advice, and please come to visit us again!" finished Ali.

You can use these questions to talk about this book with your family, friends and teachers.

What did you learn from this book?

Describe this book in one word. Funny? Scary? Colourful? Interesting?

How did this book make you feel when you finished reading it?

What was your favourite part of this book?

download our reader app
getlibraryforall.org

About the contributors

Library For All works with authors and illustrators from around the world to develop diverse, relevant, high quality stories for young readers. Visit libraryforall.org for the latest news on writers' workshop events, submission guidelines and other creative opportunities.

Did you enjoy this book?

We have hundreds more expertly curated original stories to choose from.

We work in partnership with authors, educators, cultural advisors, governments and NGOs to bring the joy of reading to children everywhere.

Did you know?

We create global impact in these fields by embracing the United Nations Sustainable Development Goals.

libraryforall.org